CW00742622

A Priest's Guide to Hospital Ministry

Edited by
Fr Peter Michael Scott

*All booklets are published thanks to the
generous support of the members of the
Catholic Truth Society*

CATHOLIC TRUTH SOCIETY
PUBLISHERS TO THE HOLY SEE

Contents

Nihil Obstat: Terry Tastard
              Diocesan Censor

Imprimatur: ✠ Vincent Nichols
              Archbishop of Westminster, 10th March 2017

Other than Cardinal Nichols, each chapter has been written by a serving healthcare chaplain. The prayers at the end of the book have all been submitted by healthcare chaplains of Westminster Diocese.

All rights reserved. First published 2017 by The Incorporated Catholic Truth Society 40-46 Harleyford Road London SE11 5AY Tel: 020 7640 0042 Fax: 020 7640 0040 © 2017 The Incorporated Catholic Truth Society.

ISBN 978 1 78469 183 7

The Redemptive Quality of Suffering

A Spiritual Reflection

One of my mother's favourite sayings was that God never gives a cross without the backs to bear it. She insisted on the plural 'backs' and not the singular 'back'. She knew that we cannot cope alone. This is particularly true at times of sickness and the pain of illness. As she knew well, at those times we need to walk together, carrying each other's loads, giving generous helping hands, soaking up frustration, promising prayer and actually doing it. Carrying the cross of illness is tough. We need each other.

Sickness and the pain of illness are part of most peoples' lives. Some seem to have more than a fair share. Others are blessed with a robust constitution! But the distress of illness comes our way at some point. What might weigh heavily with us can be the actual pain; or the frustration of not being able to do what we are used to doing; or the experience of having to rely on other people for simple things like getting out of the bath. And we all react rather differently.

Then, too, there is the experience of having someone we love caught up in illness, or incapacity, especially if the road is long and the care we want to give very demanding. We can find ourselves at our wits end, tired out and not knowing how to continue coping.

These are among the most difficult experiences of our journey of life, Yet they take us to the very heart of the summons of faith about how we are to live. St Paul puts it very powerfully: "We are well aware that God works with those who love him, those who have been called in accordance with his purpose, and turns everything to their good" (*Rm* 8:28).

This is the high point for which we are to strive: that God can turn to good all that happens to us, all that we suffer, all that bears down so heavily upon us. This is the high point: our total and peaceful acceptance that we are in God's hands, like clay in the hands of the potter; and that God is fashioning us, through sickness, into a new shape. Here God is turning everything to good, not simply my own individual good, in heaven, but the good of everyone involved in this refashioning, in which so much is stripped away and we are emptied out.

Some people attain to this understanding and acceptance of their suffering. Their faith is so deep and well tested. They usually show a most remarkable peace and even become more concerned about the well-being of others rather than their own pain. Most of us do not. We struggle in the foothills. We try to make the best of what is happening, in terms of our faith and the practical help we offer to each other.

One step is to see ourselves walking the same path as Jesus. We can try to be one with him in our heart and mind. Indeed, with encouragement we can truly offer up our suffering to our heavenly Father, in union with Jesus, for all the needs of the world. That really brings home the point and power of our morning offering each day!

In this way we try to see how God might indeed be using my suffering for a good purpose. But often that good intention can slip away in the pain and confusion we experience. For some the road is slow, it seems so long, it seems to have no end, no purpose. Jesus, too, cried out; and more than once. "Father, if it is possible let this cup pass me by" (*Mt* 26:39); "My God, my God, why have you forsaken me?" (*Mt* 27:46)

At these moments, the words of St Paul become even more important. Here, too, in moments of despair, the Father is turning all things to our good. He was "making all things new."

This is the only way: to cling on, in the knowledge that as we are emptied of our very selves, we are being made new, ready to be filled with the fullness of God's gift which is unutterable joy and light.

St Paul tells us that all this is the work of the Holy Spirit, the power of God who lifted Jesus from the tomb of death and who will lift us too into the glory of God. He says:

The Spirit too comes to help us in our weakness, for, when we do not know how to pray properly, then the Spirit personally makes our petitions for us in groans

> that cannot be put into words; and he who can see into all hearts knows what the Spirit means because the prayers that the Spirit makes for God's holy people are always in accordance with the mind of God (*Rm* 8:26-27).

Our "groans", our painful incoherent words, the cry of Jesus from the cross, all make perfect sense to our Father because it is his work that is being accomplished and Spirit that is crying out in us.

I spoke once with Cardinal Hume when he was full of the pain of his final illness. He said, distressingly: "I cannot pray! I cannot pray! All I can do is simply look at the crucifix." And there, of course, he would see Mary. He would know that she walks every step of this way of pain with us. As, in our illness, we whisper the prayers of the Rosary, we know that she is gently taking us closer to her Son and quietly bringing him to us. She is, after all, the Comfort of the Afflicted and the Health of the Sick.

Holy Mary, Mother of God, pray for us sinners, now and at the hour of our death. Amen.

Cardinal Vincent Nichols

Some Advice When Visiting a Patient in Hospital

Fr Peter Michael Scott

Be prepared to wash your hands
In these days of superbugs our appearance and willingness to follow infection control guidance is important. When visiting a hospital make sure you look smart and tidy, if possible leave your overcoat in the chaplaincy department and make sure you wash your hands before and leaving every patient and ward.

If you have hospital ID, then wear it
If you are a regular visitor to hospital and on the chaplaincy "on call" rota then you should have signed a voluntary contract and are entitled to an identification badge. This reminds staff and patients that you are legitimate visitor and someone they can trust.

Look for signs and posters either before or when visiting a patient
Most hospitals will notify visitors by posters if the patient has low immunity and infection control measures are in place. Posters which are displayed before entering a cubicle or a room will tell you to wash your hands and wear

protective clothing. Some posters above a patient's bed may indicate that they are "Nil by Mouth" and therefore should not eat anything or that they have fluid restrictions and cannot drink without the permission of a nurse. As a rule you should never help a patient to eat or drink. If in doubt always ask a nurse.

Always introduce yourself

This may sound like obvious advice, but it is so important. If you do not know the patient it confirms whether you are the person asked for. Sometimes communication in hospitals breaks down and a patient may have asked for someone of another Christian tradition or faith. Secondly it is always polite and thirdly it gives a patient the chance to focus if they are drowsy or battling with the effects of medication.

Always try to sit on a chair

Assuming the patient wants you to stay, now look for a chair and sit down. This is partly because the patient's bed is part of their small world and rather personal to them. Also you never know what lurks beneath the blanket. Catheters and drains are the common enemy, and you do not want to cause the patient any more pain than is necessary.

Never fully draw the curtain or shut a door

Sacraments and confidential chats sometimes work better if the patient does not feel as if they are being observed by the rest of the ward. Always ask the patient's permission to shut a room door or to draw the cubicle curtain. However never fully close them. We must remember that many patients are still strangers to us, and we to them. If ever you feel vulnerable with a patient or their relatives, ask a nurse to remain with you, while you visit.

Let the patient set the agenda

We must never suppose that patients want to talk about religion. We must let them set the agenda for the conversation. Sometimes they may talk about the most ordinary event just to perceive what we are like. Other times they may go straight to the heart of what is troubling them. More often than not they will talk about their relationship with God, but the art of chaplaincy is to listen closely to what they are saying and to sensitively work with them to get to the reason as to why they want to talk.

Give Holy Communion with care

Always be sensitive to the needs of the patient and wash your hands before beginning the rite of Holy Communion. If you feel the patient cannot take a whole host be prepared to split the sacrament into a smaller piece.

Do not be afraid to laugh or to smile

We are judged by our appearance not just by patients, but healthcare staff who may wish to talk to us. Having a happy disposition makes us less threatening and easier to approach.

When visiting a ward, always greet the staff

Never forget we are priests to staff as well as patients. The beauty of a hospital is that you meet staff from all faiths and none. This can be incredibly enriching and challenging. Remember, most healthcare staff hear so much negativity and criticism they will appreciate a safe pair of ears to let off steam and to ask for prayers.

Always let the Hospital Chaplain know that you have visited

Hospital chaplains are graced with the support they have from the local clergy. A really helpful discipline is to notify the employed Roman Catholic Hospital Chaplain if you have anointed one of your parishioners, or been to visit them. To ensure confidentiality, either attempt to speak to the chaplain or, if using an email, convey the ward, the bed number and the initials of the patient, but never record their full name in writing or text.

You always need the patient's permission

If you are in the habit of praying for the sick at Mass, you must ask the patients permission to convey their name to the parish in the bidding prayers or in the parish newsletter. Failure to do so could risk breaking the confidentiality policy of the hospital.

Pray

St Vincent De Paul wrote, "Give me a person of prayer, and such a one will be capable of accomplishing anything". It goes without saying that priests should pray, but it is no harm to be reminded that it is only through contact with the Father that our minds are inspired to listen intently and to answer with his words of love and encouragement. Sometimes a flicker of Scripture will illuminate our minds to be imparted to the patient or to reassure us. This is privileged work, and for many patients we are the ones who give encouragement for them to let go and to step into the loving embrace of the Father.

Anointing the Sick – a Reflection and Some Dos and Don'ts

Fr Peter Harries OP

Sickness has always troubled the human spirit. The Gospels frequently recount stories of Jesus loving sick people by visiting them and healing them. Jesus left his Church the sacrament of anointing for priests to administer God's healing grace, as documented particularly in the Letter of James. The following are a few practical reflections on administering the sacrament and visiting the dying.

Who can be anointed?
Any baptised Catholic who is seriously ill or dying, and who has reached the age of reason, unless they manifestly persist in grave sin.

How do I anoint?
There are two parts to the sacrament, the laying on of hands in silence, and the anointing with oil with the prescribed words. Always do both, unless you have just administered the sacrament of confirmation, in which case the laying on of hands is omitted. If you do not have access to the oil of the sick and the person is imminently dying, then the ritual permits the priest to bless olive oil.

Can I wear gloves?
If the sick person is infectious or prone to infection, nurses will suggest wearing gloves and other protective items. When laying on hands, hold your hands over but not on the person's head. Then dip your uncontaminated thumb into the oil stock for the anointing. If you need to use more oil, use a finger, don't risk cross-infecting the oil in your stock with your contaminated thumb. Wash your hands thoroughly afterwards.

Which parts of the body do I anoint?
Anoint the person's head first and then the palms of their hands, while saying the prescribed words. If you can't, because of bandages, blood, etc., then either omit the physical anointing or (better) anoint nearby. The ritual additionally permits the anointing of the affected part, although it would be highly prudent to avoid anointing certain areas of the body. A priest is anointed on the back of his hands, not on the palms where he was anointed during his ordination.

Should I tell the Hospital Chaplain?
If you anoint someone in hospital or a hospice please tell the chaplain. It may avoid him being called in urgently later by other family members.

How seriously ill should the person be who requests anointing?
Before the reforms of Vatican Council II, anointing was reserved to people who were dying. This understanding is

still widespread amongst many people. Vatican Council II restored an older tradition, that we anoint not only the dying but also those who are seriously ill. Before or during any illness requiring a stay in hospital or a hospice, anointing is probably appropriate. Frail (often older) people may be anointed at any time, even if no serious illness is currently threatening them.

How often should I anoint someone?
If a person's medical condition seriously deteriorates following an initial anointing, it is always appropriate to anoint them again. However try to avoid a situation where a person who is in hospital is anointed many times within a few days by different visiting priests. A frail person might be anointed once or twice a year, perhaps during a special Mass for the sick.

Can I anoint a person with psychiatric issues?
Yes, but don't anoint them frequently.

Can I anoint someone who has died?
No. The sacraments are for the living, not the dead. If a nurse or doctor tells us someone is dead, respect that information. The ritual provides prayers for a visit to someone who has just died.

What about a patient who is brain dead?
If a patient is still breathing with assistance and the doctors are telling the family that someone is brain-stem dead (or similar), then anoint the patient.

The family of an unconscious patient have asked me to anoint them. Should I?
Yes, unless you are clear that it would not be the patient's wish.

The patient is apparently living in an irregular relationship. Should I anoint them?
Yes, unless you are clear that it would not be the patient's wish.

Can I anoint Church of England people or those of other Christian communities?
Normally quite definitely no, because most Church of England (and other Christian) patients don't have a Catholic understanding of this sacrament. We must respect the integrity of faith of other non-Catholic Christian communities. Do always offer to pray for the dying person and their family.

However, there may be rare occasions when an Anglican minister is not available, the dying patient is from an Anglo-Catholic background and has a Catholic understanding of the sacraments, and the patient (or their family) spontaneously request the sacrament. In such a case a priest may absolve and anoint such a patient.

What about seriously ill or dying catechumens?
Catechumens should be baptised, confirmed, receive Holy Communion (if able) and then be anointed, in this order.

Why don't we anoint babies?
Baptised babies and small children clearly under the age of reason are assumed to be living lives innocent of sin. The sacrament of anointing asks God for the forgiveness of personal sin, and so is inappropriate for babies. Instead use the rite for visiting a sick child which includes making the sign of the cross on the child's forehead.

Can we anoint children?
Children aged seven and over, are assumed to have reached the age of reason and should be anointed. Children under seven who may have reached the age of reason should be anointed. There are special prayers in the ritual for anointing children and young people. Following appropriate catechesis, a sick or dying child may receive their first Communion at an earlier age than usual, and also be confirmed.

What about a baby who has died?
No, rather consider a blessing and naming of the child.

I am not sure if the patient is actually Catholic, or that they are penitent, or that they have reached the age of reason, or that the illness is serious
If in doubt, anoint.

Care of the Dying

Fr Peter Michael Scott

"I'm afraid I've feared death, but I won't fear it after it takes place: I'm sure of this!" These words of St Therese of Lisieux are very encouraging, very normal and often said in different ways by those who are dying. How we approach death and die can be very different, as unique as ourselves, but as St Therese says, it is about "falling into God's arms!"

As priests it is important that we have explored and thought about our own deaths
There is that old but valid exercise, where you imagine yourself dying and what might be your prayer. Hopefully you are familiar with the Scriptures to know those pieces of text which give you comfort and hope. Sometimes it can be enormously reassuring to speak these scriptural texts when the dying express their worries and fears. Those that come to mind are "Trust in God still, and trust in me, there are many rooms in my Father's house", or when Jesus spoke to the good thief from the cross he said "today you will be with me in paradise." These are beautiful words from Jesus and remind us that God will not leave us homeless at the end of our lives.

Be prepared for anger, guilt, disbelief or questions
Some patients may have supressed these and it can be very effective to encourage them to talk. To listen and be non-judgemental is the best approach. It is important the patient has a chance to express their anger or frustration. Eventually, if you judge it helpful, reading and praying some of the psalms, particularly where the psalmist expresses his frustration with God, may allow the dying to realise that others have felt the same and expressed it to the Father, enabling them not to feel guilty: Psalm 31:9-12 is particularly beautiful.

**When caring for the dying it is important
to appreciate that time is precious**
Where once patients might have been able to hold long conversations, now a few minutes might tire them out. Dying patients can sometimes become quite professional at being able to express their need or anxiety very swiftly. Be sensitive to their battle to stay awake, and do not engage them in any conversation or long liturgy which might tire them. Most rites have a shorter form.

**It is valuable to be up to date and informed about
how to organise a funeral**
On the whole, it is often the older generation who will ask, once they have received the sacraments, about their funeral. Sometimes they will have a very clear understanding of what they want, and others will have a sketchy outline. Often,

family and friends have found this conversation difficult, so a patient may feel relieved they can talk about this with you.

Dying can be a slow process

The body has been programmed to live, and if someone is expiring of a disease or of old age it may take time for the body to shut down. Often when visiting someone who appears unconscious, they will respond to touch or being spoken to. They might not be able to respond clearly, but by a flicker of their eyelids or the slight grip of a hand they will make their presence known. So a clear piece of advice is always speak and chat with the patient whether they are conscious or unconscious.

At every moment with the dying, be prepared to pray with and bless them

The sacraments of reconciliation, viaticum and anointing are integral to the journey of the dying, but there often comes a stage when the patient is unconscious and everything has been sacramentally administered. These are occasions when you stand beside the patient's bed, introduce yourself, say some words of encouragement and then gently whisper into their ear some of the sentiments and scriptural phrases contained in the chapter titled "Commendation of the Dying" from the *Pastoral Care of the Sick*, and then end with a simple blessing marked on their foreheads. This simple approach may enable the patient to let go and die.

Accompanying the dying is important, but so is our attention to their relatives and friends

Simple gestures, like talking to the unconscious patient, and blessing them on the forehead can give encouragement to visitors to speak and reach out and touch the person who is dying. Talk to them about how their loved one is important to them, and what they have achieved together. Listen to their stories and reflections and memories. Be sensitive to their wariness of you; they might not have had the chance to talk to a priest other than a greeting on a Sunday, and so they will be getting to know you and at the same time be in the first stages of grieving. If it feels appropriate, pray with them, and if it does not, then as you leave their company, remind them that you will be praying for them and the person who is dying.

Visit the dying as often as you can

The Gospel narrative that comes to mind is that of Mary of Bethany as she poured expensive perfume on Jesus's feet as she anticipated his death. Was this a waste of precious resources, or would this gesture of love inspire the Church to expend valuable resources on those who are about to die? Pastoral care of the dying is God's way of pouring his extravagant love on his creation whilst it awaits re-creation. It is through the journey of death that we are able to experience the fullness of God's love and the abundance of life that he has in store for us.

Finally, follow-up mechanisms, such as mentoring, debriefing and supervision

These are vital to nurture, support and develop you in this work. They allow a subconscious data bank of useful experiences to be built upon, from which you can intuitively draw during future encounters.

It is also appropriate to gauge a theological perspective by prayerfully reflecting on whether this work would endorse Jesus's ministry. This pastoral care in hospital does reflect his priority for the interests of the sick, lonely and the dying (*Lk* 4:18-19). It follows his example of coming close to people and involving himself in the intricacies of their lives, always tailoring his language to suit their situations and bring comfort, challenge and hope.

Ministering to Those with Mental Health Issues and Dementia

Deacon Anthony Clark

There are two important aspects of a priest's support of someone with a mental health problem. On the one hand a priest can provide appropriate support to someone with a mental health problem. On the other hand a priest should know the boundaries between what support he can offer and those of trained professionals. It is good for a priest to develop understanding and confidence on how best you can support parishioners with a mental health problem.

The first point to make is that mental health problems are the commonest of all health problems and a rough statistic today is that one in four adults will develop a mental health problem at some point in their lives, ranging in degrees of seriousness and in length of time of being affected by it.

Mental health problems range from anxiety disorders and panic attacks of one sort or another to conditions such as paranoia, schizophrenia, depression, eating disorders and various other psychotic and personality disorders.

If you recognise that someone may be affected by one of these conditions even if you don't know very precisely what it is, there are general guidelines about your next steps.

- Acknowledge how the person is feeling.
- Listen sensitively.
- Use open questions: how, what, when, where, who, why.
- Use a reassuring tone and display responsive body language.
- Avoid focussing on negative options or language.
- 'Reflect back' information.
- Don't be afraid to say, "No".
- Acknowledge a person's anger even if unfairly directed at you.
- Present any advice you give as a series of options.

It is important for every priest to know the local resources available. Signposting is a process where a parishioner is offered alternatives which they choose. It's important to be cautious in what alternatives to propose as the very naming of a resource or agency can come across as judgemental.

A priest has to know fairly precisely whether he can offer any time at all to a parishioner who asks to come and see him from time to time. A particular difficulty can arise when someone realises that a priest will nearly always try to accommodate someone who seeks the sacrament of reconciliation, and who then uses the occasion for a lengthy recounting of all their troubles.

A priest also needs to know about dementia, its various manifestations, and what local support is available. Family members will approach him with stories about particular persons they are concerned about in their family. Again, having a list of local dementia resources and contacts is invaluable to the priest in terms of signposting.

For so many adults today the biggest problem can be around lack of family and human contact. The parish is for many people the place par excellence of social interaction. This interaction is often the means for stabilising, if not being the solution to, so many mental issues. So the priest along with a parish social committee, looking to provide a variety of social occasions in the parish, is perhaps providing the most important response needed to help people with mental health problems. The priest especially is in a unique position to introduce people to each other, nudging along a new relationship with a hint of how somebody could be helped. It is very similar to a priest's role in helping somebody who is grieving, introducing them to somebody who has had a similar experience.

A priest should make sure he gets some background information and advice if he takes on visiting patients in mental health settings. There is a great need for mental health chaplains in various institutions. A priest needs to know that patient listening is so often the most important service he can give, along with the offer of the sacraments of healing and praying with the patients.

So many priests are lone occupants of their presbytery, struggling with very great demands on them. It is important to recognise that you need support and help too, especially if there are parishioners who you feel are dependent on you. In medical settings, there are systems and helps built in to provide support to doctors, nurses and care workers. You need to set up a system of a monthly session of 'supervision' where you can talk to a fellow priest or somebody similar in a setting of confidentiality, aimed not at giving you information about how to solve other people's problems but aimed at giving you the chance to talk about yourself, the issues that worry you and the chance to talk matters through.

Finally, three further helpful pieces of advice, particularly with regards to those with dementia receiving the sacraments:

1. Communication

Communication is very important issue. When visiting have plenty of time and be relaxed. Do not be too complicated. It is a real blessing to be able to enjoy the person you are with. If you know about their background talk about it with them, people with dementia remember the past much better than they remember the present. Talking about church last Sunday will remind the individual of their trips to church throughout their life. Gentle chats give a calm and relaxed atmosphere. People with dementia and some mental health disorders become distressed when they cannot understand.

They equally become distressed when they cannot work out how to reply to somebody. So it's really important to try and avoid arguments. It's also useful to try and put the answers into questions. Rather than saying, "Do you want Holy Communion?" it is perhaps a little better to try something like "it's my day for visiting you and so I brought you Holy Communion." The latter may well get a far more positive response.

2. Holy Communion

To receive Holy Communion requires the proper dispositions for receiving Holy Communion. It also requires an understanding and belief that this is something special. In the case of someone with learning disabilities it would only be necessary to establish that they knew the difference between the Eucharist and ordinary bread – "a belief that is it something special". As a result it may not be suitable for those with very severe dementia and it can be problematic for people who spit it out. Generally one is likely to assume that if people spit out the host they are failing to understand what is offered. If you were to ask a person who is a devout Catholic whether they would wish to continue receiving Holy Communion if they reached a point where they unwittingly spat out the sacred host, they would surely say that they would not wish to receive in those circumstances. This is not a question of a person being "unworthy" but of respecting the dignity of someone who has always lived a devout Catholic life. Shorter readings and prayers can also be a good idea.

3. Reconciliation

Confession requires an awareness of sin, an understanding of repentance, and the ability to articulate both the sins and the repentance. Consider offering confession to those with early dementia who are Catholic rather than forgetting the spiritual needs of our patients until it is too late. It is worth mentioning that people do some remarkably inappropriate things when they have dementia. Perfectly decent kind and saintly people will start hitting, spitting, swearing and stripping off. These are almost certainly not sins. They are not wilful acts but they reflect acts of disordered minds and we may console ourselves and their families with the thought that they are done in the innocence of dementia.

Paediatric Chaplaincy

Anne Marie O'Riordan

"Jesus said, 'Let the little children come to me, and do not hinder them, for the kingdom of heaven belongs to such as these.'"(*Mt* 19:14)

Interaction

In all encounters with children, see them with God's eyes and enable them to feel God's great love. Engage with the child no matter how young, affirming their dignity and worth. Be gentle and considerate with your words.

When relating to children I find it helpful to open with general chit chat, i.e. how old they are, guess their school year, ask them how school is going, etc. Take the time to establish some trust and then ask them what they would like to say to God. Wherever possible give children a voice. If you visit a child with severe physical and cognitive disabilities, be aware of the importance of non-verbal communication. Touch, facial expressions, mirroring and sensory feedback are important communication tools. As with all physical contact, always ask the family and the child for permission beforehand.

Prayer

It can be difficult to enable children to relate to God personally using words alone. Harness the power of children's imagination. Just as Jesus spoke in parables using strong narrative images, symbols and pictures can convey meaning simply.

The Lord's Prayer is pivotal for me. I encourage children and families to focus on the line "Give us this day our daily bread" as a way of asking God to give them what they need for that day. When children and families feel overwhelmed they are often reassured that God already knows what they need and this helps them to surrender.

Finally, I try not to be afraid to accompany parents as they enter the darkness and pain of their situation. Sometimes prayers and words are insufficient. Be patient and willing to take the time to listen and not fill in the silence. This can help parents and children to express themselves or simply feel held by God.

The sacraments

Baptism

When baptising a child on the ward, adhere to the same infection control standards mentioned earlier. Do not use holy water. Ask nursing staff to give you some cotton wool, a bottle of sterilised water and an aluminium dish. Pour the water into the dish and set aside. You will bless and make the water holy as part of the rite.

Wards are not set up for rituals so you may have limited space for religious paraphernalia. My baptism kit includes laminated baptism orders of service, a baptismal candle (do not light on the ward due to fire risk), an electric candle (can be lit instead), a baptism certificate and baptism details form (in case you need to ask the local parish church to issue the certificate). Unless it is an end of life situation or if the family have been given permission, do not lay white linen on the child (infection control). Enter the baptismal details into the hospital register or ask the RC Hospital Chaplain to do this.

When baptising a baby in an incubator, you may not be able to access their head due to lines and other medical equipment. Using cotton wool simply soak this in the holy water and pour three drops onto the most accessible part of the body, e.g. hand or foot.

Communion

It is especially comforting, strengthening and healing when I take a family member or child through this ritual in a prayerful way. Children often receive Communion more openly when they feel they are sharing a meal with Jesus and see him at the table with them. You may also discover that family members have not received Communion for a long time. Be aware that some parents may feel guilty about issues in their lives and may interpret their child's sickness as a form of punishment.

End of life

As a priest you will play a crucial role in the care of a dying child, at the point of their death and after they die. You may be involved in helping a child come to terms with their imminent death (wish lists can be helpful as conversation openers). In my experience, children accept that they are dying earlier than family members, often holding out until parents are ready to say goodbye. It is their way of protecting mum and dad. Children like honesty and the truth. Don't dress up the truth, give it to them straight but with kindness.

Withdrawal of treatments can be challenging. I have discovered that ritual can help parents to transition psychologically and let go. Recently, I was gifted some large purificators embroidered with the cross and occasionally, with permission from the family, I will lay one on the child during a withdrawal. I normally place an electric candle on top plus some rosary beads. This simple act signifies to the family that their child belongs to God and is now returning home.

You may also be asked to visit the mortuary to bless a child. Usually, there will be a special viewing bedroom. A good mortician will place a child in a comfy bed and ensure they are dressed in their personal clothes with favourite toys or other items around them. Furthermore, families may ask you some difficult or pointed questions such as, "Where is my child now?", "Are they missing me?", "Did they go to heaven alone?", "Does the Catholic Church allow cremation?", "Can I keep my child's ashes at home?"

Self care

Paediatric hospital ministry can drain you emotionally so find ways to look after yourself. Receive supervision and see a spiritual director regularly, find your own way of processing events. Make time for prayer and do the things you enjoy.

Some Helpful Medical Ethics

Fr Giles Pinnock

Admission to hospital brings many uncertainties and fears. There may be issues around the morality of the treatments for which a Catholic patient is being asked to give their consent. Medical staff should be assumed to be of good will and good intention; however, the treatments they recommend may not be consistent with the teaching of the Catholic Church.

Parish priests should be equipped to offer advice to their parishioners, often in immediate crisis, or know to turn for that advice to the bishop, or the Catholic Hospital Chaplain. It is important to remember that, save in an emergency, no medical procedure can be carried out without the informed consent of the patient or their legally empowered representative, and that no patient should ever be coerced by any person into giving consent for treatment that they do not want.

IVF (*in vitro* fertilisation)

It is a tragedy for a couple who are unable to conceive naturally, and such a couple must be cared for pastorally with compassion, while remembering that children are

God's gift alone and there is no right to parenthood. It is likely that IVF treatment, using the husband's sperm and the wife's eggs, or those of donors may be suggested However, IVF is not consistent with the Church's teaching.

IVF will almost always result in 'surplus' embryos, which may be frozen for future use should the first attempt at IVF be unsuccessful or if further children should be desired. Alternatively, they may be destroyed should genetic abnormalities be detected or if the couple ultimately decide they do not want further IVF treatment. Each of these 'surplus' embryos are a child of the parents no less than those who are allowed to be born, and no less deserving of their love. The process of IVF does not allow them their human dignity.

IVF invades upon the married love of the husband and wife, and potentially upon the right to life of any human being conceived in this way. Infertile couples may better be counselled to offer their love and their homes through fostering and adoption to children without parents able to care for them – in which they may experience great fulfilment.

Abortion or termination of pregnancy

The sanctity of life is directly denied in abortion – the procedure has one intended outcome, the death of the child in its mother's womb – which is never morally justifiable, and which carries the penalty of automatic excommunication for anyone involved.

A mother may be told that her child has abnormalities incompatible with life or which are likely to result in significant disability, and strongly advised that she should consider ending her pregnancy. Even in such circumstances, abortion is not morally justifiable. While the child is alive in its mother's womb, his or her abnormalities are not incompatible with life at that time. Even if the child would not be expected to live for very long once born, he or she is morally entitled to the fullest span of life naturally possible, despite the challenges which may arise through disability. A mother faced with such a situation should be supported by her parish priest in continuing her pregnancy to its natural outcome, and in particular in welcoming and bringing up her child.

Ectopic pregnancy – when a fertilised egg implants outside the womb, meaning that the child can never come to birth and that the mother's life is threatened – appears to present a particular challenge. Unless it is treated, the mother will die, but removal of the embryo would appear to be an abortion.

Most moral theologians accept is that it is moral to treat an ectopic pregnancy surgically. There is an opportunity to verify that there is indeed an ectopic pregnancy which threatens the mother's life, and if so, the embryo and the mother's surrounding tissue are removed with the direct intention of saving the mother's life, indirectly but unavoidably resulting in the death of the embryo.

Suicide/euthanasia

Faced with the possibility of a difficult death, a patient may request that their doctor assist them to end their life. It is never morally justifiable for a doctor intentionally to end a patient's life, nor for a patient to request them to do so.

However, doctors are not morally obliged to offer every possible life-prolonging treatment if they do not believe that they would serve the patient's best interests, nor is the patient morally obliged to accept any treatment that might be offered, particularly if they feel that it might result in disproportionate suffering. To refuse potentially life-prolonging treatment for good reason does not constitute suicide/euthanasia.

Nutrition and hydration

The Catholic Church holds that the provision of hydration (water) and nutrition (food) is a basic human right. The medical profession generally holds that when nutrition and hydration has to be provided artificially, it becomes a treatment that can ethically be withheld. The family of a patient nearing the end of their life may find that artificial nutrition and hydration is to be withdrawn, and fear that the patient is being subjected to a form of euthanasia.

Families should be supported in asking for justification for the withdrawal of hydration and nutrition. Although as the patient nears the end of their life, artificial hydration and nutrition may cause harm, they may have been withdrawn because they are believed to be futile. Families should be supported in requesting the maintenance of hydration and nutrition, unless it can be shown that they would certainly cause the patient harm.

DNAR (Do Not Attempt Resuscitation)

To be told that medical staff do not intend to resuscitate a loved one should their heart or breathing stop can be deeply distressing, particularly if this information is not communicated well. Families may well feel that this amounts to euthanasia.

When a patient's heart or breathing stop, this is naturally part of the process of dying. Resuscitation can be a very physical treatment, resulting in bruising, broken bones, and the administration of electric shocks to someone who is already very frail, very often with a limited probability of a successful outcome. While the family of a patient who is not to be resuscitated should be supported in asking for justification of that decision, they may also need to be helped to understand that death is naturally part of human life and that when its moment comes, it should be accepted, in sorrow, but also in faith in the resurrection.

Some Useful Prayers and Liturgies

Prayers before visiting the sick

Heavenly Father,
You have made us to love you and
    to love our neighbours.
So often, we think only of ourselves,
    and overlook those who are in need.
Lord, you never ignore us, but are always
    eager to save us.
Help us to be more like you, to love others
    as you love us.
May we never disregard those who are vulnerable,
    but seek to do your will,
through Christ our Lord. Amen.

Fr Peter Michael Scott

O God of the ever present crosses,
help us, your servants.

Fourth century, Egypt

God's might to uphold me,
God's wisdom to guide me,
God's eye to look before me,
God's ear to hear me,
God's word to speak for me,
God's hand to guard me,
God's way to lie before me,
God's shield to protect me,
God's host to secure me,
Christ to protect me today. Amen.

St Patrick

Prayer after visiting the sick

Lord,
Thank you for each person I have visited today
    in your name.
I hold each one up to you now.
You know their need.
Bless them with all the blessings they need.
Heal them to wholeness in body, mind and spirit.
Comfort and console them and give them the gift of
    fortitude – your strength for the journey they are on.
Grant them the peace and joy of your presence,
    hope in your help and faith in your love. Amen.

Some prayers with patients

Soul of Christ, sanctify me. Body of Christ, heal me.
Blood of Christ, drench me, Water from the side of Christ,
wash me. Passion of Christ, strengthen me. Good Jesus,
hear me. In your wounds shelter me. From turning away
keep me. From the evil one protect me. At the hour of my
death call me. Into your presence lead me, to praise you
with all your saints for ever and ever. Amen.

Prayer to Christ the healer

In the comfort of your love,
I pour out to you, my Saviour
the memories that haunt me,
the anxieties that perplex me,
the fears that stifle me,
the sickness that prevails upon me,
and the frustration of all the pain that weaves
about within me.
Lord, help me to see your peace in my turmoil,
your compassion in my sorrow,
your forgiveness in my weakness,
and your love in my need.
Touch me, O Lord, with your healing power
and strength.

Take Lord
and receive all my liberty,
my memory, my understanding and my will;
all that I have and possess you have given to me;
and to you I give it all back.
It is all yours;
Dispose of it according to your will.
Give me only your love and your grace;
this alone suffices for me.
St Ignatius of Loyola

———

Be still and be comforted; the Lord is with you,
strengthening and supporting you.
Put your trust in him for he loves and cares for you.
Listen to Jesus when he says, "Peace be still" and
    believe that he is with you, and will help you always.
Harold Winstone

———

Let nothing disturb you, let nothing affright you. All things
are passing. God never changes. Patient endurance attains
to all things. Who God possesses, in nothing is wanting.
Alone God suffices.
St Teresa's Bookmark

God, grant me the serenity to accept the things
    I cannot change,
courage to change the things I can and wisdom
    to know the difference:
living one day at a time, enjoying one moment at a time;
accepting hardship as a pathway to peace;
taking, as Jesus did, this sinful world as it is,
    not as I would have it;
trusting that you will make all things right if
    I surrender to your will;
so that I may be reasonably happy in this life and
supremely happy with you for ever in the next. Amen.
Reinhold Niebuhr

My Lord God,
I have no idea where I am going
I do not see the road ahead of me
I cannot know for certain where it will end.
Nor do I really know myself, and
the fact that I think I am following your will
does not mean that I am actually doing so.
But I believe that the desire to please you
does in fact please you.
And I hope I have that desire in all that I am doing.
I hope that I will never do anything apart from that desire.
And I know that if I do this you will lead me
    by the right road

though I may know nothing about it.
Therefore I will trust you always
though I may seem to be lost and in the shadow of death.
I will not fear, for you are ever with me,
and you will never leave me to face my perils alone.
Thomas Merton

Blessing of patients in a hospital bay

Lord, our God,
who watch over your creatures with unfailing care,
    keep us in the safe embrace of your love.
With your strong right hand raise up your servants
    N. and N.
And give them the strength of your own power.
Minister to them and heal their illnesses, so that they may
    have from you the help they long for.

We ask this through Christ our Lord. Amen.

Blessing of an individual patient

Lord and Father, almighty and eternal God,
by your blessings you give us strength and support
    in our frailty:
turn with kindness toward this your servant N.
Free him/her from all illness and restore him/her to health,

so that in the sure knowledge of your goodness he/she will gratefully bless your holy name.

We ask this through Jesus Christ our Lord Amen.

Prayer for doctors and nurses

O merciful Father, who have wonderfully fashioned man in your own image, and have made his body to be a temple of the Holy Spirit, sanctify our doctors and nurses and all those whom you have called to study and practise the arts of healing the sick and the prevention of disease and pain. Strengthen them in body and soul, and bless their work, that they may give comfort to those for whose salvation your Son became man, lived on this earth, healed the sick, and suffered and died on the cross. Amen.

Blessing for carers' hands

This simple act can be done at the end of Mass, after the final prayer.

Invite those who care for the sick to come forward and present their hands with their palms facing upwards.

To anoint, use some holy water and make a small sign of the cross in the palm of the other person's hands saying: "May God bless your hands for healing."

When all assembled have been blessed finish with this simple acknowledgement:

Yours are the hands full of experience and skill.
Yours are the hands reaching out with compassion,
taking time to show care, swiftly taking action.
Yours are the hands gently touching your patients.
You touch families, too.
Yours are the hands that show you care.
You lift the hearts of those who suffer.
Your hands celebrate the joy of healing.
Your hands bless all they touch with the spirit
   of compassion,
thank you for sharing your abundance and gifts,
for touching lives and lifting spirits.
Blessings and thanks for the many works of your hands.
May your hands bring healing to all those you touch.

As St Teresa of Avila says:

Christ has no body now but yours. No hands, no feet on earth but yours. Yours are the eyes through which he looks [with] compassion on this world. Yours are the feet with which he walks to do good. Yours are the hands through which he blesses all the world. Yours are the hands, yours are the feet, yours are the eyes, you are his body. Christ has no body now on earth but yours. Amen.

Then finish Mass with final blessing.

The Rite of Anointing the Sick

Introductory Rites

Greeting

The Priest approaches the sick person and greets him and the others present in a friendly manner.

"The peace of the Lord be with you always"

R. And with your Spirit.

Instruction

Then the Priest addresses those present in these or similar words:

Lord God you have said to us through your apostle James: 'Are there people sick among you? Let them send for the priests of the Church, and let the priests pray over them anointing them with oil in the name of the Lord. The prayer of faith will save the sick persons, and the Lord will raise them up. If they have committed any sins their sins will be forgiven them.' Lord we are gathered here in your name and we ask you to be among us, to watch over our brother/sister N. We ask this with confidence, for you live and reign for ever and ever,

R. Amen.

Liturgy of Anointing

Laying on of hands

In silence the Priest lays his hands on the head of the sick person.

Anointing

The Priest takes the oil and anoints the sick person. He anoints first on the forehead, saying:

> Through this holy anointing may the Lord in his love and mercy help you with the grace of the Holy Spirit.

> R. Amen.

Then on the hands, saying:

> May the Lord who frees you from sin save you and raise you up.

> R. Amen.

The Lord's Prayer

The Priest introduces the Lord's Prayer in these or similar words:

> At the Saviours command and formed by divine teaching, we dare to say:

> (All say) *Our Father…*

Prayer after Anointing

The priest may say:

Father in heaven, through this holy anointing grant N. comfort in his/her suffering.
When he/she is afraid, give him/her courage.
When afflicted, give him/her patience,
when dejected, afford him/her hope,
and when alone, assure him/her of the support of your holy people.
We ask this through Christ our Lord.

R. Amen.

Concluding Rite

Blessing

The priest will conclude by blessing the patient saying:

May the blessing of almighty God, the Father, and the Son, and the Holy Spirit, come upon you and remain with you for ever."

R. Amen.

Apostolic Blessing

The current ritual of the anointing of the sick states that the priest "may add the apostolic pardon for the dying" after the penitential rite or after the sacrament of penance."

The Apostolic Blessing has two forms in the ritual for the anointing of the sick. Both are short and easy to memorise. Form A: "Through the holy mysteries of our redemption, may almighty God release you from all punishments in this life and in the life to come. May he open to you the gates of paradise and welcome you to everlasting joy."
Form B reads as follows: "By the authority which the Apostolic See has given me, I grant you a full pardon."

Prayer before Communion to be repeated with someone with dementia

Lord Jesus, come to me.
Lord, Jesus, give me your love.
Lord Jesus, come to me and give me yourself.
Lord Jesus, come to me.
Lord Jesus, you are my Lord and my God.
Praise to you, Lord Jesus Christ. Amen.

Prayer for carers of those with dementia

O Lord we pray for all those whose work is dedicated to the assessment and care of those who experience confusion and profound memory loss.
For all who are carers or work as healthcare professionals

in everyday care and research into the causes of
dementia of many kinds.
May they be strengthened in their work of service
with individuals, families and friends.
Through Jesus Christ our Lord. Amen.
Fr Edward Pogmore

Prayer for those with dementia

Lord, thank you for your presence,
this moment, holding us in your love.
Help us to share your love with those who live
among us with dementia,
that we may see your beauty in them. Amen.

Prayer to Our Lady of Mental Peace

Mother of tranquillity, Mother of hope,
Our Lady of Mental Peace,
we reach out to you for what is needful in our weakness.
Teach a searching heart that God's love is unchanging,
that human love begins and grows by touching God's love.
Let your gentle peace be always with us and
help us to bring this same peace into the lives of others.
Our Lady of Mental Peace – pray for us.

Prayer for those in mental torment

Be still and be comforted; the Lord is with you,
strengthening and supporting you.

Put your trust in him for he loves and cares for you.
Listen to Jesus when he says, "Peace be still" and believe
that he is with you, and will help you always.
Harold Winstone

Do not look forward in fear to the changes in life;
rather, look to them with full hope that as they arise,
God, whose very own you are,
will lead you safely through all things;
and when you cannot stand it,
God will carry you in his arms.

Do not fear what may happen tomorrow;
the same understanding Father who cares for
you today will take care of you then and every day.

He will either shield you from suffering
or will give you unfailing strength to bear it.
Be at peace,
and put aside all anxious thoughts and imaginations.
St Francis de Sales

Dedication of a child to Mary

Mary, Mother of God, take this child under your tender
care. Watch over him/her always. Grant that his/her
journey through this world may lead to eternal life. We ask
this through Christ our Lord. Amen.

Prayer for a new child

Loving God, giver of life, you call each of us by name: thank you for the gift of this new child. Bless him/her with your grace and love. May he/she grow in wisdom, knowledge and truth and may your love embrace him/her always. Amen.

Blessing for new parents

Loving God, bless the parents of this new baby. Keep them safe all the days of their life. Grant them wisdom, peace and many years of joy with their child. Amen.

Prayer for a sick baby

Lord, we pray to you for this baby who is sick.
If it is your will, grant that he/she may be brought to perfect health. Amen.

Alternative liturgy for someone near to death

Dear N.
Loved and known by God. Loved and known
    by your family and friends.
We have come to be with you, to thank God for you,
    to pray with you and for you and to accompany you as
    you prepare for the next stage of your spiritual journey.
Jesus promised that where two or three are gathered in
    his name he would be present.

A selection of readings from the Old Testament

Do not fear, greatly beloved. Be strong and courageous (*Dn* 10:18).

—◊◊◊—

Strengthen all weary hands, steady all trembling knees and say to the faint-hearted: "Be strong. Do not be afraid. Here is your God…he is coming to save you" (*Is* 35:3-4).

—◊◊◊—

Rejoice because God has remembered you, walk safely in God's glory…God will guide you in joy by the light of his glory…[and carry] you gloriously to his royal throne (*Ba* 5:1-9).

A selection of psalms

I lift up my eyes towards the mountains from whence shall help come to me. My help is from the Lord…the Lord is beside you…the Lord will guard you from all evil…the Lord will guard your coming and your going, both now and for ever (*Ps* 121).

A compilation of psalms

The Lord's my shepherd, I'll not want. He makes me down to lie in pastures green. He leadeth me the quiet waters by. Though I walk in death's dark vale, yet will I fear none ill.

For thou art with me and thy rod and staff me comfort still.
Goodness and mercy all my life shall surely follow me and
in God's house for evermore my dwelling place shall be
(*Ps* 23:1-2,4,6).

—◈◈◈—

…I went with the throng…in procession to the house of
God, with glad shouts and songs of thanksgiving (*Ps* 42:4).

A selection of Gospel readings

The Lord Jesus says, "I go to prepare a place for you, and
I will come again to take you to myself" (*Jn* 14:2-3).

—◈◈◈—

"I am the resurrection and the life," says the Lord. "Those
who believe in me, even though they die, will live"
(*Jn* 11:25-6).

—◈◈◈—

I am with you always (*Mt* 28:20).

—◈◈◈—

This day you will be with me in paradise (*Lk* 23:43).

—◈◈◈—

Remember me when you come into your kingdom (*Lk* 23:42).

—⁓—

Take heart, your sins are forgiven (*Mt* 9:2).

—⁓—

"Come, blessed of my Father," says the Lord "and take possession of the kingdom prepared for you" (*Mt* 25:34).

—⁓—

At last, all powerful Master, you give leave to your servant to go in peace, according to your promise. For my eyes have seen your salvation which you have prepared for all (*Lk* 2:29-30 the Canticle of Simeon).

—⁓—

Into your hands Lord, I commend my spirit (*Ps* 31:5 and *Lk* 23:46).

Loving God, may your Holy Spirit come upon N. now and strengthen him/her (pause).

Let us pray for your loved ones, for those who are here with you now and for those who would like to be here but are unable to be.

Thank you, Lord, for the love and care of family and friends. It's hard to say, "Goodbye". Be with them in the good times and in the hard times. Comfort and console them in their grief. Bless them with a life of love, peace and joy lived in union with you and each other. Amen.

Let us join hands together and say:

Our Father… Hail Mary… Glory be…

May the grace, mercy and peace from God the Father, the Son and the Holy Spirit be with us always (*1 Tm* 1:2). Amen.

Death

"A priest started his homily at a funeral by saying, 'I am going to preach about judgement.' There was dismay in the congregation. But he went on: 'Judgement is whispering into the ear of a merciful and compassionate God the story of my life which I had never been able to tell.' It is a very great encouragement to think of being in the presence of God who is both merciful and full of compassion, because God knows me through and through and understands me far better than I could ever know and understand myself, or anyone else. Only he can truly make sense of my confused and rambling story.

Death is not the end of the road,
but a gateway to a better place.
It is in this place that our
noblest aspirations will be realised.
It is here that we will understand how
    our experiences
of goodness, love, beauty, and
joy are realities which exist
perfectly in God.
It is in heaven
that we shall rest in him and our hearts
    will be restless until they rest in God."
Cardinal Basil Hume

O Lord, support us all the day long
until the shadows lengthen and evening comes,
and the busy world is hushed,
and the fever of life is over,
and our work is done.
Then, in your mercy,
grant us a safe lodging,
and a holy rest, and peace at last.
Cardinal Newman

To you, O Lord,
we humbly entrust N.
so precious in your sight.
Take him/her into paradise,
where there will be no sorrow,
no weeping or pain,
but the fullness of peace and joy
with your Son and the Holy Spirit
for ever and ever. Amen.
Order of Christian Funerals

Some Useful Websites

For helpful guidelines and policy:
http://www.cbcew.org.uk/CBCEW-Home/Departments/Christian-Responsibility-and-Citizenship/Health-and-Social-Care

For resources regarding assistance with those suffering from dementia:
http://www.pastoralcareproject.org.uk/dementia-prayer-week.html

Resources and materials to support those who are dying:
http://www.artofdyingwell.org/

For baby or neonatal deaths:
https://www.sands.org.uk/

For up to date guidance on medical ethics:
http://www.bioethics.org.uk/

Has this book helped you?
Spread the word!

@CTSpublishers

/CTSpublishers

ctscatholiccompass.org

Let us know!
marketing@ctsbooks.org
+44 (0)207 640 0042

Learn, love, live your faith.
www.CTSbooks.org